IMAGES
of America

BOSTON POLICE
BEHIND THE BADGE

On June 10, 1923, Boston Police patrolmen of the riot squad with their riot rifles show their skills on the Boston Police range located at Fort Standish in Boston Harbor. Lt. Louis E. Lutz was the commander of the training; and range instructors Sgt. Thomas S.J. Kavanagh of headquarters, drillmaster patrolman Frank Tays of Station No. 4, and patrolman William H. Evans of Station No. 16, and patrolman Edward E. Seibolt of Station No. 15 assisted Lieutenant Lutz. (Courtesy of Boston Police.)

ON THE COVER: From left to right, Capt. John F. Petiti (not pictured), patrolman Edward Silver, patrolman James Welch, and Sgt. Det. Mark Madden of Station No. 11, Dorchester, look over the recovered loot taken from three homes early in the morning on January 27, 1959. The stolen property was valued at $2,500, and it was later learned that the stolen property was actually from a total of 45 different homes. Boston Police arrested a juvenile and were looking for two of his accomplices. (Courtesy of Boston Police.)

IMAGES
of *America*

BOSTON POLICE
BEHIND THE BADGE

Robert E. Anthony
for the Boston Police Department
Foreword by
Commissioner Edward F. Davis

ARCADIA
PUBLISHING

Published by Arcadia Publishing
Charleston, South Carolina

Library of Congress Control Number: 2012944775

For all general information, please contact Arcadia Publishing:
Telephone 843-853-2070
Fax 843-853-0044
E-mail sales@arcadiapublishing.com
For customer service and orders:
Toll-Free 1-888-313-2665

Visit us on the Internet at www.arcadiapublishing.com

This book is dedicated to the men and women, past, present, and future, who have put on the fabric of a Boston Police officer.

CONTENTS

FOREWORD

Boston's proud law enforcement history predates our nation's history by 150 years. While Boston's role in America's political and cultural development are well known, the contributions of the Boston Police Department to the city and to the development of American law enforcement are less well documented. This book contributes to that knowledge.

The story of the Boston Police Department (BPD) has perhaps best been told by our own, from works by 19th-century police chief Edward H. Savage to Images of America: *Boston Police Department* by Donna M. Wells. Ofc. Robert "Bob" Anthony's *Boston Police: Behind the Badge* follows in that tradition. In his role as the department's first chronologist, Bob Anthony has gathered and shared our history within the department and with the public. This book, in words and images, brings his work to a wider audience.

When Boston Police boast we are "first in the nation," we are looking back to our roots in the Boston Watch of the Towne of Boston in the 1630s. The current structure of the BPD dates to 1854. Over the course of nearly four centuries, the city has increased in geography and in population, and the Boston Police Department has grown and matured to meet the needs and challenges of a great metropolis. In this volume, you will meet some of the officers who served with distinction through the years. Among these are our first African American officer, appointed in 1878, and the first women police officers, appointed in 1921.

The tools of policing have also changed. Our harbor patrol started with a few rowboats. Our K-9 unit began 50 years ago, and our motorcycle unit started a century ago. This book includes handsome photographs of our storied mounted unit, which, in its era, served a vital role.

Boston has had its share of celebrations and turmoil through the years, and the Boston Police were part of this history. Whether during the national unrest of the 1960s or the Boston school desegregation of the 1970s, the BPD answered the call. Of course, in 1919, it was the police officers themselves who made history with the Boston Police Strike, which shook the city and started Gov. Calvin Coolidge on the road to the White House.

No cop can reflect on the success of an organization without remembering those officers who gave their lives in service. They are remembered here and are always in our hearts.

Scripture tells us "there is nothing new under the sun." A newspaper headline about political terrorists directing bombs at Boston Police could describe the 1916 anarchist attacks in Boston's North End as well as the terror of April 2013. And the men and women of the Boston Police Department, like their predecessors, stand prepared to prevent and protect. These pages tell our story.

—Police commissioner Edward F. Davis
Boston, Massachusetts, 2013

ACKNOWLEDGMENTS

This project could not have happened without the help of the dedicated people at our nation's first police department over the years. This book is the result of efforts of officers who came before me; they passed on old photographs and valuable tidbits of information to me. They have provided a window into our department's history. I would like to mention the following people and groups for their assistance and guidance throughout this process. I would first like to recognize my wife, Jacalyn Anthony, who has been my rock; my daughter, Carrie; grandchildren, Kayla, John, Jacqueline, Nicolette, and Alexandria; and son-in-law, Phillip Brangiforte. I thank also Mayor Thomas Menino and Commissioner Edward F. Davis who conferred this position to me with the understanding of just how important our history is. Thanks go to Det. Richard Devoe and police officer William Carroll, the Boston Police Relief Association, the Boston Police Patrolmen's Association, Boston Police Superior Officers Federation, and Boston Police Detectives Benevolent Society for their support. Thanks go to Margaret Sullivan, police officer Danny Cunningham, and police officer Kevin Egan, Superintendent-in-chief Daniel Linskey, Supt. William Evans, Supt. William Gross, Joseph Favale, and retired captain Robert Cunningham. My appreciation goes to the Boston Police Emerald Society, Boston Police Honor Guard, Boston Police Gaelic Column; Lt. Hervey Cote; Boston Transportation Department (BTD) commissioner Thomas Tinlin, Steven Wysocki, Paul McColgan, and Willie Dupree of BTD, who worked on our Boston Police Hero Signs projects; Kathy Kearney and police officer Q. Riley of the BPD Commissioner Office; Michael Simmons and Billy Goodwin of the BPD Central Supply Office; Caitlin O'Rourke, Greg Mahoney, and the BPD Graphics Department; and police officer Jamie Kenneally in public relations. My gratitude also goes to all the families of our fallen officers; "we will never forget our fallen." If I missed someone, I apologize.

Unless otherwise noted, all images appear courtesy of the Boston Police Department.

INTRODUCTION

American law enforcement can trace its roots to Boston and the Boston Police Department. The citizens of the town of Boston established a watch in 1631; the town took command of the watch in 1636. Watchmen patrolled at night on foot, looking for criminals, undomesticated animals, Indians, and fire. Their duties grew along with the metropolis, which, in 1822, became known as the city of Boston. In 1838, Boston recognized a police force of six men under the command of a city marshal. The Boston Watch of 120 men operated independently.

On October 6, 1851, Mayor Bigelow nominated Barney McGinniskin as the first person of Irish heritage ever selected as a police officer in Boston. When the anti-immigrant, anti-Catholic Know-Nothing Party took control of the Massachusetts state government in 1854, McGinniskin was fired, and Boston was again without an Irish police officer.

In 1854, the old police and watches were abolished and structured into the Boston Police Department with 250 officers. Each officer was paid $2 per day or night shift, he could not hold any outside employment, and each officer walked his own beat. These officers were issued a bill and hook and a rattle to sound the alarm or call for assistance. Later, the bill and hook of the old watch was replaced with a 14-inch club.

In the late 19th century, Boston Police provided benevolent services. Police officers at each station would serve soup to the underprivileged—first at the expenditure of the officers themselves and later with funds from the city. Newcomers to Boston could spend a night as a dweller in a police station. Police ambulances/wagons would transport sick and injured citizens to Boston City Hospital.

Boston used stagecoach wagons, which were called the "Black Mariah" as they were mostly used to transport persons under the influence from the bars in Downtown Boston. The name came from boardinghouse owner Maria Lee, a large black woman who, in the 1820s, was feared more than the police; the police would ask her to help them detain and restrain criminals. Thus, the name Black Mariah was given to the wagon. These wagons were horse drawn with two horses, a wagon master, and rider. The department has one of these wagons in its historic collection.

Boston took over several neighboring towns in the 1870s and directed police services to these territories. Phone lines replaced the telegraph system that linked the central office with all police houses. Police call boxes were installed all over the city in the 1880s. The call boxes were easy to access with a key by officers on their beats; the officer would have to turn the key to let the station know that he was on patrol or on his rounds. These call boxes had a light on top that would flash to let the police officer know that the station was trying to get a hold of an officer on his beat. The officers would have numerous calls boxes on their walking beats to turn within a certain time, and if an officer missed a box, a wagon would be sent out to check on his well-being. If an officer had to take a suspect into custody, he would first have to drag the suspect to the call box and then ring the box for a wagon to transport the suspect back to the station.

On December 24, 1878, the first African American officer, Horatio Julius Homer, was appointed to the Boston Police Department; he served our department and the citizens of Boston for 41 years, retiring in 1919. Homer achieved the rank of sergeant.

At the beginning of the 1900s, the department employed 1,000 patrolmen, who made about 32,000 arrests annually. Police officers' duties now included monitoring motor vehicle traffic, issuing citations, removing disorderly passengers from streetcars, and inspecting City of Boston permits at the open-air markets in Haymarket Square.

One of our highest decorated officers was patrolman George H. Nee, who was appointed to the Boston Police Department in 1901. While serving his country in the US Army, Private Nee was awarded the Medal of Honor for assisting in the rescue of those wounded on the front lines while under heavy fire from the enemy in Cuba in 1898.

Our very first police automobile was purchased in 1903; it was a Stanley Steamer. Our first patrol wagon, which also doubled as an ambulance, was purchased in 1912. In 1912, motorcycles were used for the first time for traffic control; two officers in District No. 4 put them into use. Commissioner Stephen O'Meara saw the immense demand for these motorcycles and ordered another six to be put into service. Police motorcycles (mobile patrol) were used to deal with the ever-increasing traffic and the enforcement of the motor vehicle laws. Motorcycles could be used for parades and demonstrations, and they could cut in and out of traffic to get to a location faster than a car.

The police strike of 1919 made nationwide headlines and changed the department, which replaced nearly three-quarters of its police force. To fill the ranks, the department recruited returning war veterans. In the 1920s, the department dealt with Prohibition and crimes that came along with it. A police officer's pay at the time was $26.81 a week with one day off in eight; an officer was also paid 60¢ per court appearance. This was an especially deadly time for the Boston Police Department, with 16 officers killed in the line of duty between 1920 and 1930. Another 14 police officers were killed in the line of duty from 1930 to 1940. The Depression brought a smaller city budget and a cut in police pay. During World War II, many officers left the department for several years to join the military.

Like many police departments in the 1960s, the Boston Police Department was called upon to safeguard order during periods of protest and disorder. With the local introduction of school desegregation in 1974, the department deployed officers throughout the city to escort schoolchildren and their buses to various schools in the city and ensure public safety. The Boston Police Department Tactical Patrol Force (TPF) was used to handle security throughout the city. Most officers were forced to work nonstop without time off.

To meet the demands of 21st-century policing, the department built a state-of-the-art facility in 1997. While earlier police headquarters were near the centers of Boston government and businesses, the new Boston Police Headquarters is near the geographic core of the city in the Roxbury district. One Schroeder Plaza Boston Police Headquarters is named for brothers, patrolman Walter Schroeder and Det. John Schroeder, both Boston Police officers killed in the line of duty on September 24, 1970, and November 30, 1974, respectively.

Boston's pledge to community policing has noticeably reduced crime and has been studied by police departments across the nation. It is one of the foremost police departments in the nation. From transformation to police administration and communications in the 19th century to innovative expertise and strategies today, the Boston Police Department continues to protect and to serve to all Bostonians and to act as an example to all the nation's police departments.

One

BEHIND THE BADGE

In 1873, Boston Police officers stand outside Division No. 15, Charlestown. Officers are wearing the fifth-issued Boston Police badge (the silver dollar), used from 1870 to 1879 and designed by Chief Edward Hartwell Savage (chief from 1870 to 1878).

Boston Police patrolmen stand outside Station No. 4, Boylston Market. This photograph was taken in December 1901.

Pictured in 1915, Boston patrolmen are standing outside Station No. 14, Brighton, which also houses today's municipal court. At this time, there were only about seven African American policemen in Boston; note the African American police officer second from the left in the second row.

Here, Boston patrolmen, along with Boston Fire Department personnel, assist in locating victims of an explosion of illuminating gas in the subway at the intersection of Tremont and Boylston Streets on March 5, 1897. Six people died in this explosion, and scores were injured. Buildings in all directions were damaged by the concussion, and several electric cars that were passing at the time were wrecked. One caught fire and was burned to the tracks. The property damage amounted to thousands of dollars. This disaster was by far the worst of its kind ever known in Boston.

Pictured on May 10, 1922, Sgt. Thomas S.J. Kavanagh and Lieutenant King instruct officers of the riot squad in rifle training on the range, which is located on Lovell's Island in Boston Harbor.

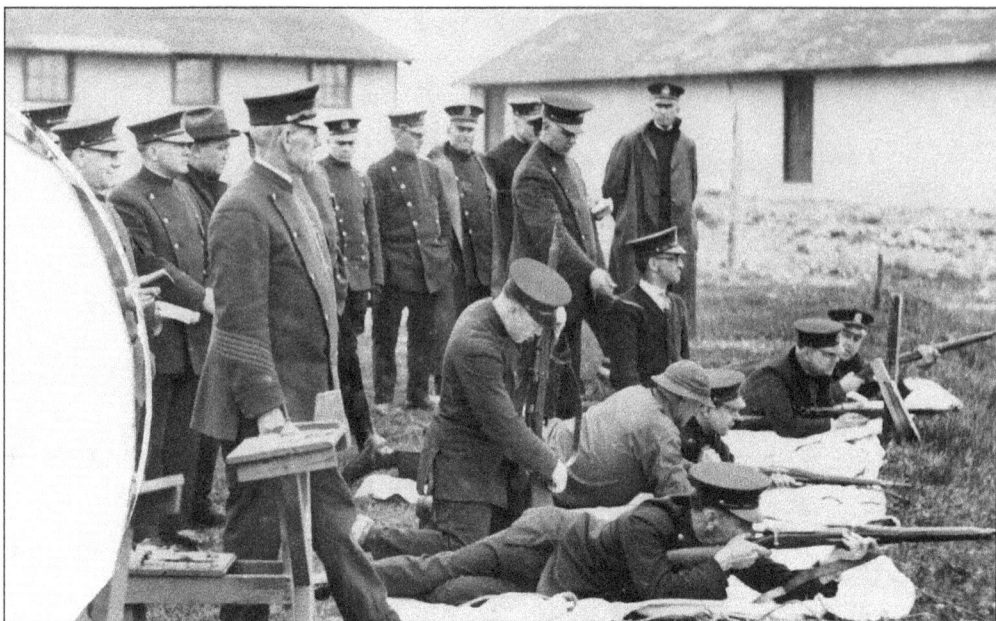

On Lovell's Island on May 10, 1922, range instructors, under the direction of Lieutenant King and Sergeant Kavanagh, teach rifle marksmanship to the Boston Police patrolmen.

Here, Lieutenant King and Sgt. Thomas S.J. Kavanagh check the targets of the patrolmen at the range on Lovell's Island. These patrolmen were part of the riot squad of the Boston Police Department.

Sgt. Horatio Julius Homer was the first African American officer in the Boston Police Department. He joined the department on December 24, 1878. In September 1895, he was promoted to the rank of sergeant. Sergeant Homer retired on January 29, 1919, at the age of 71, having served the city of Boston and Boston Police Department for 41 years and one month. He passed away on January 12, 1923. Research by Margaret Sullivan and police officer Robert E. Anthony found that Sergeant Homer and his wife, Lydia, were buried in an unmarked grave in the Evergreen Cemetery in the Brighton section of Boston. This information was brought to the attention of police commissioner Edward Davis and Mayor Thomas Menino, who directed both Sullivan and Anthony to see what could be done to correct this dishonor. The department and community came together to collect funds, and a proper burial with honors was given to Sergeant Homer and his wife, Lydia. Also, a headstone was installed, and over 400 officers along with family and friends attended the ceremony.

Sergeant Horatio Julius Homer
First African American Boston Police Officer
Appointed December 24, 1878
Retired Jan 29, 1919

Edward Hartwell Savage was appointed to the Boston Police Department in 1851. Three years later, he was promoted to captain and took command of District No. 1, Downtown Boston. In 1861, Savage was appointed deputy chief. In 1870, he was made chief of police. During the 1860s, Savage introduced a rogues' gallery, the first traffic squad, the civil service regulations, and the Boston Policeman's Ball. He was one of Boston's most popular police chiefs and proved to be a knowledgeable realist who championed precautionary policing and rehabilitation before they were trends. He also designed some of the Boston Police's first-issued badges, including the fourth-issued urn badge in 1868 and the fifth-issued silver dollar badge in 1870. In 1878, Savage left policing to become the city's first probation officer. His emphasis on rehabilitation had an intense impact on the establishment of the 1870 National Prison Association and the founding of the International Association of Chiefs of Police (IACP).

Capt. Louis E. Lutz of the Boston Police Department Riot Squad inspects the pistols of the oncoming shift at Boston Police Headquarters in Pemberton Square in 1924.

Seen here on September 5, 1936, a patrolman directs traffic from his traffic box on State Street. In the rear is the old state house, which is decorated in flags, rosettes, bunting, and a huge reproduction of the Harvard University seal with its motto "Veritas." Harvard was celebrating it 300th anniversary under the direction of the State Street Committee.

On March 3, 1932, Supt. William Crowley examines a letter that was mailed to the Boston Police Department addressed to Col. Charles A. Lindbergh. The letter directed Lindbergh to seek his kidnapped son in a house in New Jersey near the scene of the crime. Also pictured with Superintendent Crowley are postal inspectors and detectives who immediately launched a search for the woman who mailed the letter. Charles Augustus Lindbergh Jr. was the son of famous aviator and his wife, Anne Morrow Lindbergh; he was abducted from his family home in East Amwell, New Jersey, on the evening of March 1, 1932. His body was found two months later a short distance from the scene of the abduction. A medical examination determined that the cause of death was a massive skull fracture.

From left to right, Capt. R.C. Bunge of Cincinnati, Ohio, designer and builder of the famous Alcatraz prison in California; Commissioner Eugene McSweeney; police superintendent Edward Fallon; and Suffolk County Courthouse commissioner Joseph A. Rourke are pictured on October 23, 1936, discussing the temporary city tombs until the new $5 million courthouse will be erected.

Members of the Boston Police stand ready to be called into action if needed on April 26, 1968. The Boston Redevelopment Authority (BRA) was having problems at some of its locations. Over 100 patrolmen and their supervisors stand by for orders. (Courtesy of *Boston Herald*.)

Boston Police patrolmen from Station No. 6, South Boston, located on Broadway Street, are pictured on June 15, 1911. The officers are wearing the gray bobby hat, which was used in the summer months. Also, they are wearing the radiator badge, the sixth-issued badge of the Boston Police Department, used from 1879–1922.

Pictured on July 22, 1934, are Boston Police lieutenants in charge of the Teletype and Records Division of the Bureau of Operations. Here, the lieutenants would receive messages from Boston patrolmen and sent from other police departments regarding crimes and would then pass that information onto the proper department.

On February 15, 1948, "Who's Crying Now" Joseph Buckley is holding one of the new gas guns inside the armory of the Boston Police Department. The department is well stocked with plenty of ammunition.

Boston patrolmen and firemen rescue driver George Keller, who plunged 25 feet into the channel of the harbor in South Boston on April 18, 1938. Keller suffered a few scratches. Boston patrolmen are in rowboats assisting with the rescue.

Inventor Oscar L. Ely of the ballistic unit out of Boston Police Headquarters is seen with his punching machine. The machine punches a red card that is then put in an electrical device in the commissioner's office that records its information onto a huge map of Boston. Police commissioner Joseph Timilty (left) and Superintendent Fallon are inspecting the results on August 27, 1939; the map depicts the locations where crimes have happened. (Courtesy of Leslie Jones.)

On January 23, 1953, a Boston Police patrolman works in the turret at headquarters. Here, the officers receive outside calls and then relay them to the dispatch who sends them out to the radio cars.

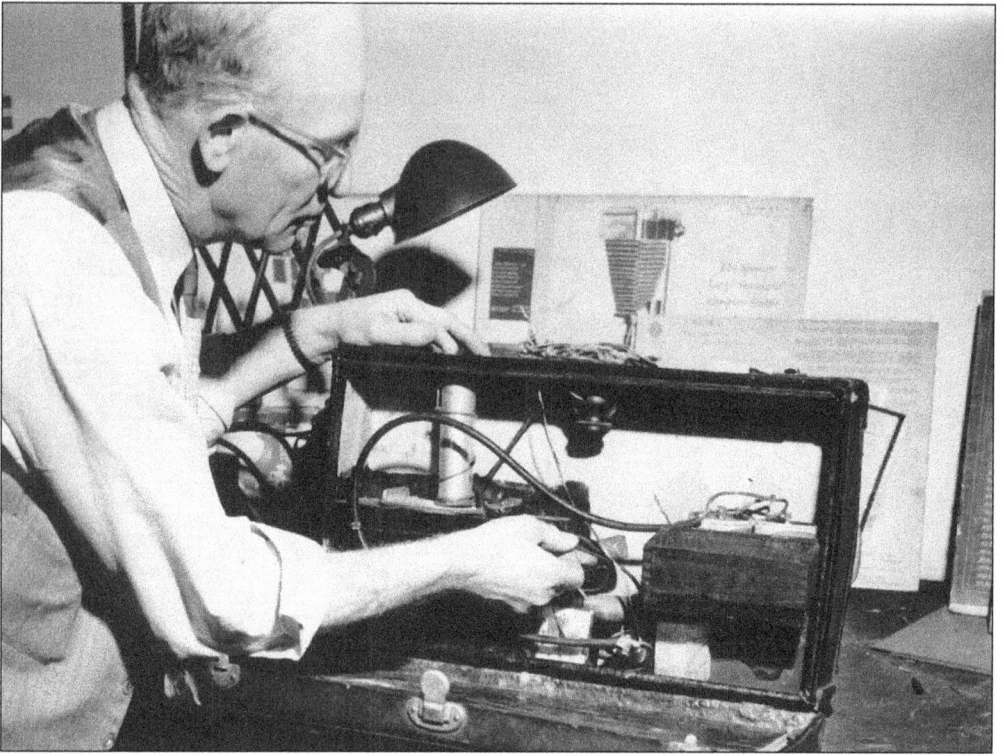

Boston Police detective Earl Laird inspects a suspicious suitcase on February 16, 1953; the suitcase was ingeniously wired to explode when the case was opened and was also timed to explode in the event no one opened it. Detective Laird was able to defuse the device.

Supt. William Taylor is shown swearing in the newest 44 Boston Police recruits at Station No. 4, Warren Street, in the South End of Boston on July 10, 1969.

On November 29, 1956, patrolmen Daniel Murphy (left) and Joseph Hurley are getting some street experience as part of their police training. They are operating a prowl car during their two weeks of indoctrination training.

Boston Police respond to a bank holdup on September 18, 1956. Four men robbed the National Shawmut Bank at Audubon Circle Branch and terrorized 18 customers and employees. The bandits escaped with $10,000.

On May 28, 1958, Commissioner Leo J. Sullivan holds up the new Boston Police patch over the old patch on the arm of patrolman John J. Cunniffe of the traffic division. The new sailboat patch took the old patch's place on June 1, 1958. (Courtesy of *Record American*.)

As of January 23, 1953, Boston Police had new radios installed in the cruisers. Officers were then able to acknowledge a call and respond to the scene.

Searching on a tip on July 1, 1951, patrolmen Walter Lindsey (left) and William Howard check the tomb in the Copp's Hill cemetery for missing Brink's robbery money from 1950. The tip was found to be false.

Seven suspects identified as participants in the January 17, 1950, Brink's robbery in Boston are shown here on January 12, 1956. From left to right are (bottom row) Thomas Francis Richardson, Joseph James O'Keefe, and Joseph H. McGinnis; (top row) Vincent Costa, Ralph Maffie, Anthony Pino, and Henry Baker.

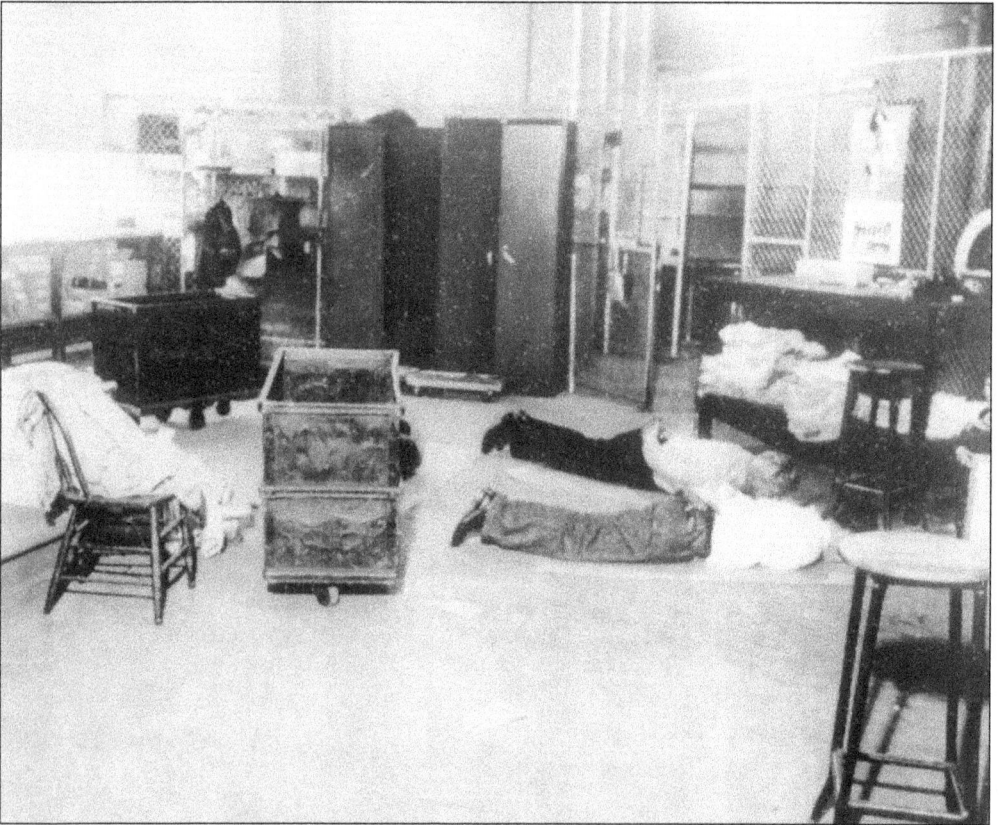

Victims of the Brink's robbery in this picture are James C. Allen, left foreground, and Sherman D. Smith, extreme right. The January 17, 1950, photograph also shows the vault at the end of the room. The suspects were apprehended in 1956, just 11 days before the statutes of limitations would have expired.

26

On January 17, 1950, victims of the Brink's robbery reenact what happened on the night the nation's biggest cash robbery occurred, when $2,775,395.12 in cash, checks, and money orders was stolen. The men tied up are those who were working that fateful night. Thomas B. Lloyd, foreground, and Charles S. Grell show how they were restrained.

Patrolman James Finnegan from District No. 7, East Boston, takes a cigarette break on November 4, 1963, after he was wounded in a bank holdup. Patrolman Finnegan suffered a flesh wound to his right arm.

Patrolman Bill Crosby shakes his billy club as he scolds a chimp through the plate-glass window of a department store in Downtown Boston on January 17, 1965. The chimp had escaped from a cage inside the store and attracted the attention of passersby when he smashed a plate-glass window. When patrolman Crosby arrived on the scene, the chimp had moved over to another window.

Here, on February 15, 1948, patrolman Edward Culkin, ballistician in charge of the Ballistic Department for the Boston Police, examines a pistol that was turned in. Patrolman Culkin runs tests on the weapon to see if it was used in any crimes.

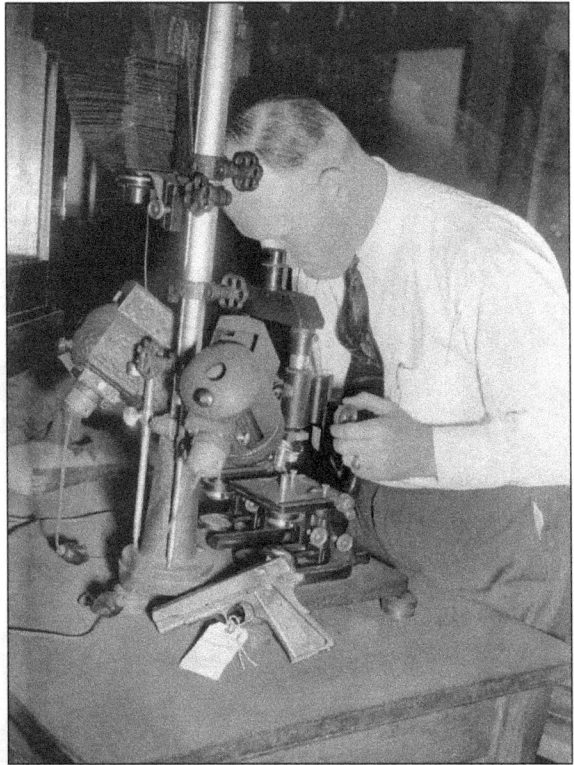

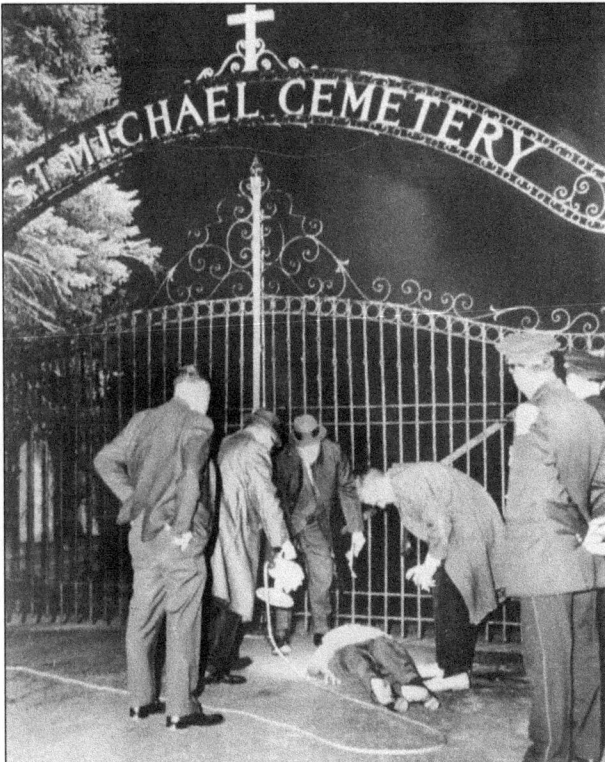

On May 22, 1967, Boston Police investigate the 44th gangland victim left outside St. Michael's Cemetery in Jamaica Plain. This was the 44th gangland killing in just the past three years. The victim was identified as Robert E. "Red" Conlin; he was described as an enforcer for the loan shark operators in Boston.

Boston patrolmen Joseph Pirrello (standing) and John Regan display $2,144 stolen from the Boston Five Cents Saving Bank at 285 Cambridge Street. Also pictured are the two pistols and pillowcase used in the bank robbery. Both officers intercepted the stocking-masked gunman. The 18-year-old Charlestown youth disarmed a guard and terrorized five employees and two customers during the robbery. Pirrello and Regan are pictured here on January 22, 1975.

Patrolman Ernest P. Hubbard walks the beat of South Boston on April 23, 1953. Boston was tabbed as the tops in security and crime prevention among the nation's largest cities. Credit for the ratings goes to the foot patrolmen.

"The Annie Oakley of the Boston Police Department," Ofc. Marie Donahue is shown on February 5, 1976, as she fires her .38-caliber pistol at the Boston Police range on Moon Island.

On February 13, 1953, Boston patrolman Francis "Frank" Schroeder of Station No. 9, Roxbury, looks over a safe that was recovered in the back alley of Dromey Street in Dorchester. The safe was stolen from the Prime Market on Blue Hill Avenue in Dorchester and broken into, and $10,000 was stolen. Schroeder would go on to become a deputy superintendent.

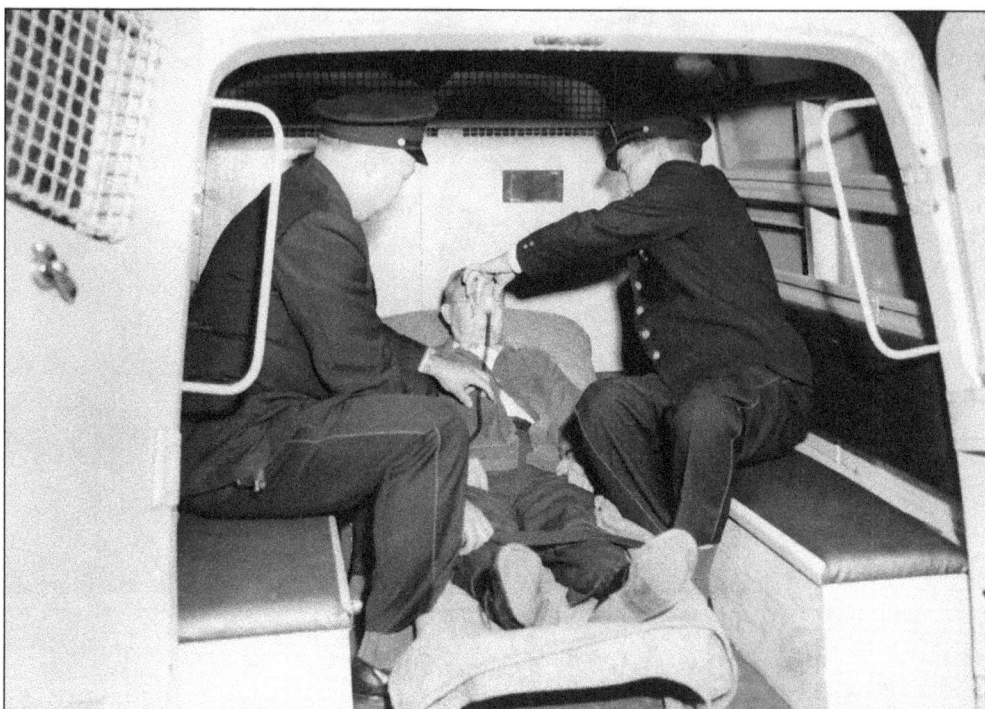

Boston Police assist a victim with oxygen as they get ready to transport him in the Boston Police ambulance to the hospital in 1941.

Police officers transport a young lady who fell in the snow at the Tremont Street train station on December 28, 1967. Patrolmen are carrying her to the Boston Police ambulance outside the Massachusetts Bay Transportation Authority (MBTA) station.

Boston traffic patrolman Walter Fahey is shown taking his lunch break in the Boston Common after a long morning directing traffic in the downtown section of Boston. This photograph was taken on March 15, 1976.

Here, on December 9, 1961, patrolman Charles McClosky speaks to Levon Kasarjian, the owner of a variety store on Dale Street in Roxbury. Kasarjian shows how the suspect, a black male, put a rope around his neck, kicked him in the leg, and then robbed his store of $30. With 35 years on the job, Patrolman McClosky is still working the beat.

Boston Police patrolmen arrest James McDougal of Dorchester on September 17, 1964. He was found inside a shipping company's building in Boston. McDougal was charged with breaking and entering. He is shown in the photograph leaping into the arms of the officers who then handcuffed him and took him into custody.

Pictured on August 28, 1964, Boston patrolmen carry the body of a woman who jumped out the window of a Tremont Street building. The victim was pronounced dead at the scene.

Here, members of the Boston Police Relief Association meet with Mayor John F. Collins in an attempt to win a pay raise in 1964. They failed to reach an agreement on a raise for Boston Police officers. Pictured are, from left to right, patrolmen Kirk Ampollos, Alfred Dello Russo, Anthony Settino, Fred Trisler, and Robert Nicholson. (Courtesy of *Record American*.)

Boston patrolmen John Patchett (left) and Richard Butler close in on 19-year-old Rosalee Smith. On June 15, 1963, the suspect had a large 10-inch carving knife she had already slashed one man with, and was menacing scores of others. The patrolmen used their nightsticks to knock the knife out of her hands and then arrested her. She was later sent to a mental hospital for observation.

Pictured here on June 26, 1968, patrolman Thomas Hogan displays the new uniform that will be worn by officers of the tactical patrol force (TPF).

Boston Police officer Shelia Kaplan works the turret at operations in 1975. She is ready to dispatch a patrol car for a call.

Pictured here in 1976, police officer Patricia Reem, the first female motorcycle officer, is writing parking tickets in Downtown Boston.

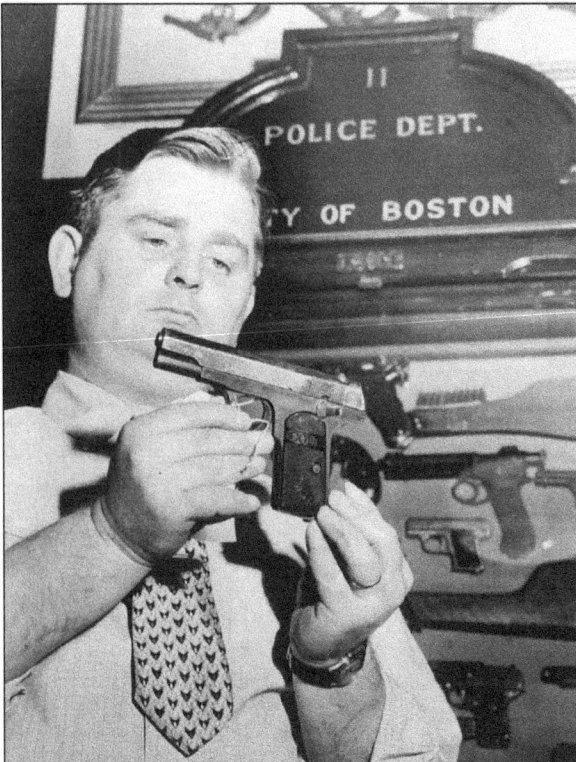

Boston Police officer Frank Bailey, a ballistics expert, is shown here on February 16, 1953, holding the weapon that killed Boston sergeant William F. Healey on October 2, 1946.

On February 15, 1948, the Boston Police Department displays weapons stored in the ballistics unit. These weapons have been removed from suspects during their arrests. Weapons include sawed-off shotguns, tiny concealed pistols, Mauser 7-point 6.3, machine pistol stock attachment, flare guns, and .45-caliber and long-rifle pistols.

Boston Police officers try to get the attention of Mayor Kevin White who is walking with his wife from city hall to Faneuil Hall for his inauguration on January 4, 1972. Officers were upset with the mayor because the lack of a new contract meant an officer was paid $5,000 less than some other city workers.

Members of the Boston Police Patrolmen's Association walk an informational picket line outside the Sheraton Plaza Hotel in Boston on March 1, 1972. The picket line was staged at a dinner Mayor Kevin White was hosting for Sen. Edmund Muskie. Officers are protesting a pay raise promise the mayor made but never kept.

In November 1972, Commissioner Robert J. DiGrazia appoints his new command staff for the Boston Police Department. Shown in the photograph of five new deputy superintendents are, from left to right, Francis Schroeder, Anthony DiNatale, unidentified, Commissioner DiGrazia, James "Jack" Barry, Paul Russell Sr., and an unidentified superintendent.

Mayor Kevin White promotes two new officers, Supt. Edward Connolly (left) and deputy superintendent Evan Bolt, to his command staff on June 22, 1979.

Boston Police promotion ceremonies are held at the municipal building in Hyde Park. Here, the newest members of the command staff walk to the front of the stage. Mayor Kevin White passed out their new badges, and family members pinned them. Family members, friends, and community members are seen standing and applauding the officers as they enter the hall.

Pictured here in 1978, from left to right, Dennis Kearney, Mayor Kevin White, Mayor White's granddaughter, Commissioner Joseph M. Jordan, and deputy superintendent Peter Donahue (far right) congratulate Lt. Louis Scapicchio (second from right) on his promotion as he will be taking over command at District No. 7, East Boston, as the acting captain.

Patrolman Marcie Corwin from District No. 11 checks a weapon that was recovered from a bank robbery in Dorchester. Money was also recovered.

Members of the Boston Police Department are pictured at roll call in the garage at Frontage Road in 1978. On the far right of the first row is Sgt. Robert Dunford, who would later become superintendent in chief of the department.

Two

HARBOR UNIT

This Boston Police harbor master patrols the harbor in the _Watchman_ on July 9, 1914.

On July 6, 1913, Boston Police Harbor Unit boat *Palm* is seen anchored. This boat was used to patrol for unmuffled motorboats on the harbor.

Seen here on July 5, 1914, is the Boston Police harbor patrol boat *Guardian*. This boat was launched on May 26, 1896, and served the Boston Police Department for more than 38 years. It was retired in 1934.

The Boston Police Harbor Unit welcomes its newest police boat, the *Stephen O'Meara*, on February 12, 1931. The boat was named for former police commissioner Stephen O'Meara, who served the Boston Police as commissioner from June 4, 1906, until December 14, 1918. (Courtesy of Leslie Jones.)

On February 12, 1931, the Boston Police Harbor Unit patrol boat *Stephen O'Meara* is out for a trial run after being christened. Aboard are members of the commissioner staff, press, and designer and builder, along with officers of the harbor patrol. In the background are East Boston and the East Boston Fishing Company. (Courtesy of Leslie Jones.)

The Boston Police boat *William H. Pierce* is searching the harbor along with the four other Boston Police boats on December 24, 1937. They are looking for the body of Army parachute jumper Harold J. Kraner, who was swept into the sea attempting to entertain the wives and children of Army airport personnel, which included his own wife and son.

Boston Police aboard the *William H. Pierce* search the harbor on December 24, 1937, for missing parachute jumper Harold J. Kraner.

Boston Police harbor master and members of the Boston Police Harbor Unit are seen aboard the *Edwin U. Curtis*. They recovered this rowboat, which had sunk in Boston Harbor.

Captain Perry, harbor master of the Boston Police Harbor Unit, takes the newest boat, *E.U. Curtis,* on its trial trip around Boston Harbor on March 15, 1931. This boat will be used to run down ship pirates in the harbor. This boat is named for former harbor master sergeant E.U. Curtis. (Courtesy of Leslie Jones.)

On July 28, 1964, the Boston Police Harbor Unit takes out its newest boat, *John F. Kennedy,* named for the former president. On the boat are members of the Boston Police Department and friends of President Kennedy.

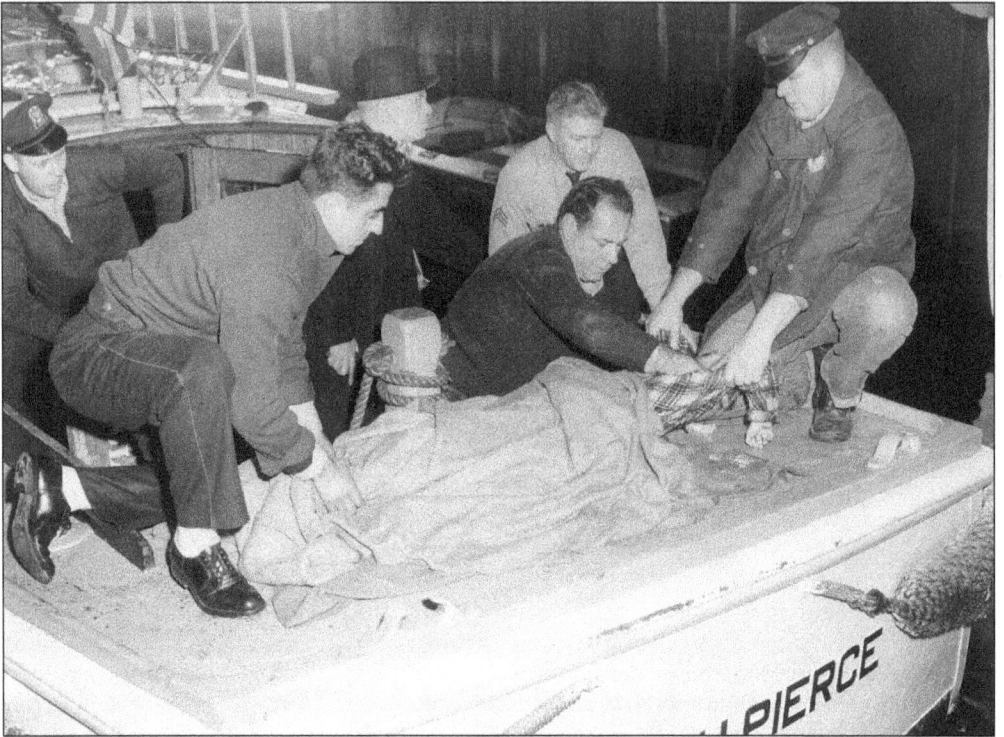

Members of the Boston Police Harbor Unit aboard the *William H. Pierce* retrieve the body of a six-year-old boy from Charlestown who, while playing, fell off the seawall along the Charles River and to his death. This event took place on November 29, 1954.

After a long day patrolling Boston Harbor on February 10, 1966, members of the Boston Police Harbor Unit dock the *William H. Pierce* for the night until the first shift takes over.

Capts. William Donovan (left), Francis X. Quinn (center), and Patrick J. O'Donnell inspect the fire damage to the police boat *Michael H. Crowley* on March 14, 1958. The inspection revealed arson, and the boat was ruled a total loss and was condemned.

When the police boat *Michael H. Crowley* was burned at its North End Pier in March 1958, the US Navy donated a former patrol craft to the Boston Police Department on July 2, 1959. This sleek 63-footer is set to patrol Boston Harbor.

Boston Police Harbor Unit patrol officers search the docks for an escaped prisoner who was a fugitive from the Charles Street Jail on May 6, 1941.

On June 26, 1961, Boston Police boat *William H. McShane* was called into action to rescue two men and a boy from Texas when their rented sailboat flipped in the wind 200 yards from Rowe's Wharf. Everyone was saved without a loss of life.

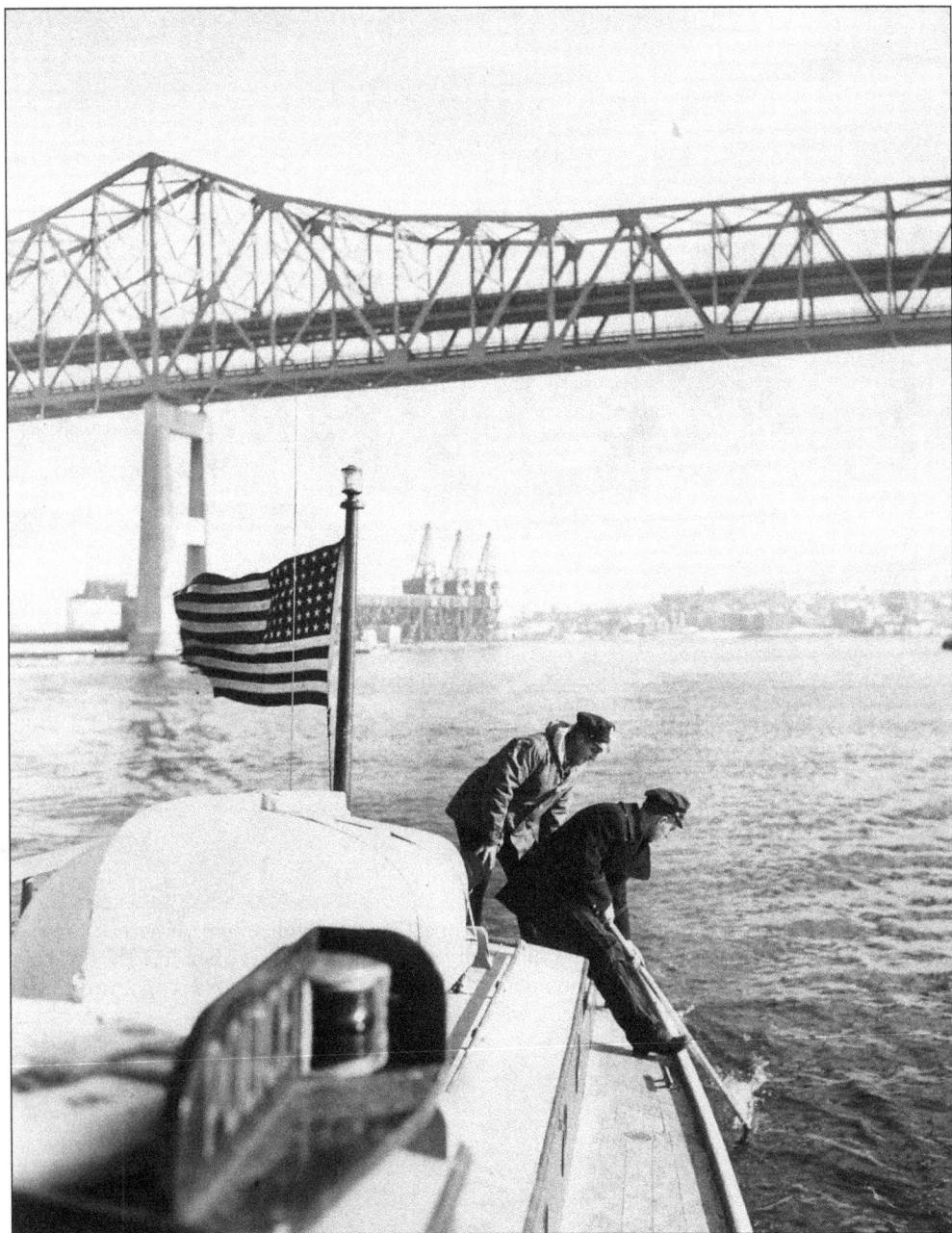

On Saturday, January 13, 1951, Boston Police Harbor Unit patrolmen Leonard Allen (left) and Thomas Gormley, aboard the *William H. Pierce*, are shown grappling for the body of a person who jumped off the New Mystic River Bridge, which is shown in the background.

Boston Police Harbor Unit patrolmen conduct an inspection of the police boat *Michael H. Crowley* on March 10, 1958, before starting their tour of duty patrolling Boston Harbor. In 1937, this boat was named in honor of former superintendent Michael H. Crowley, who was appointed to the Boston Police in 1888. Superintendent Crowley passed away in 1933.

Three

THE MOUNTED UNIT

Sgt. Edward B. Cain (far left) is in a line of Boston's finest mounted bluecoats. These mounted officers were some of the best in the country. They were handpicked by Capt. John M. Anderson of the Back Bay Division to compete in the National Horse Show at the Boston Garden. This photograph was taken on Tuesday, October 22, 1929.

Pictured on September 16, 1919, members of the military on their horses attended roll call before they were given their assignment to patrol Downtown Boston during the labor controversy of the Boston Police Department strike.

Pictured in September 1919 are two members of the military, patrolling Downtown Boston during the Boston Police strike. Note the one on the left is wearing a Boston Police radiator badge on his jacket.

On Tuesday, January 13, 1920, a Boston Police mounted patrolman is acting as the crossing guard as he makes sure the schoolchildren of the North End of Boston get to school safely.

Here, members of the Boston Police Department Mounted Unit from Station No. 16 get ready to march in a parade on December 13, 1920.

A Boston Police Mounted Unit officer keeps his eyes on the crowd and keeps the people moving along Park Street near Beacon Street in February 1932.

Here, Sgt. Edward B. Cain (on the left) is in a line of 17 of Boston's finest mounted officers. Sergeant Cain is drilling the officers and horses to compete in the October 26, 1929, National Horse Show at the Boston Garden. The Boston Police Mounted Unit finished in first place in the events and earned a gold medal. This photograph was taken on Tuesday, October 22, 1929, outside of the Commonwealth Armory.

Here is another photograph from Tuesday, October 22, 1929; it shows Sgt. Edward B. Cain (far left) lined up with the Boston Police Mounted Unit. They are going through their horsemanship drills for the upcoming National Horse Show competition.

Here, members of the Boston Police Mounted Unit have finished their training and are ready to be dismissed and head back to the barn at Division No. 16. This photograph was taken on October 22, 1929.

The Boston Police Mounted Unit is standing in front of a Christmas tree at Station No. 16, Back Bay, on December 24, 1936. L.E. Whitney, the manager of the Hotel Kenmore, presents Capt. Francis Tiernan and the horses their favorite tidbit, a bowl of sugar. Patrolman Augustus Crehan plays the role of Santa Claus. Sitting on the horse on the right is William "Pete" Dooley; he was in charge of the mounted unit and stables. The name of his horse was Vigilant. (Courtesy of *Boston Herald*.)

Pictured are members of the Boston Police Mounted Unit practicing their drills at the Commonwealth Armory on October 12, 1939.

Patrolman William "Pete" Dooley gets ready to have his picture taken by eight-year-old Nancy Burns during the March 9, 1950, Easter parade on Commonwealth Avenue.

"You wouldn't know the old place now." During the morning of June 6, 1955, on Westland Avenue and Hemmingway Street in the Back Bay, mounted patrolman Malcolm Prosser of Station No. 16 brings Toby, his thoroughbred Finger Morgan, to the old watering trough but finds it filled with flowers instead of water. So, Toby just gets a whiff of the blossoms instead of a drink of water.

Chairman Harry Blake holds the reins of mounted officer Benjamin Donoghue's horse; the two other men are, from left to right, William "Pete" Dooley and Paul Simonetti. They are getting ready to open the Christmas displays on Boston Common on December 16, 1957.

Boston Police Mounted Unit officers William "Pete" Dooley (right) and Paul Simonetti are seen outside the stables and are ready to start their tour of duty on March 17, 1960.

Pictured here on January 13, 1959, police horse Orien (center) is seen on his last day of work before retiring after 10 years of service to the department. Twenty-year-old Orien was suffering from arthritis. Saying good-bye are, from left to right, Sgt. John Lynch with his horse Dandy, Ofc. Thomas Lambert (with Orien), and Ofc. John Gallagher with Justin. Patrolman John J. Gallagher would give his life in the line of duty on May 25, 1962.

Before the start of the 1960 St. Patrick's Day parade in the Back Bay area of Boston, Commissioner Leo J. Sullivan (left) is shown talking to patrolman William "Pete" Dooley, mounted on his horse on the left, and Sgt. John Lynch. The man next to Sullivan on the sidewalk is unidentified.

On a cold winter morning, January 7, 1970, mounted patrolman Dennis Vitale and his steed, Domino, patrol the Boston Common during a snowstorm. The mounted unit was able to keep crime down on the Common because of its visibility and ability to get through the snow.

Mounted patrolman George Noonan, riding Equus, patrols Winchester Street in the Bay Village section of Boston during the morning of April 19, 1980. The high visibility of the mounted unit was able to deter the prostitute problem in the area.

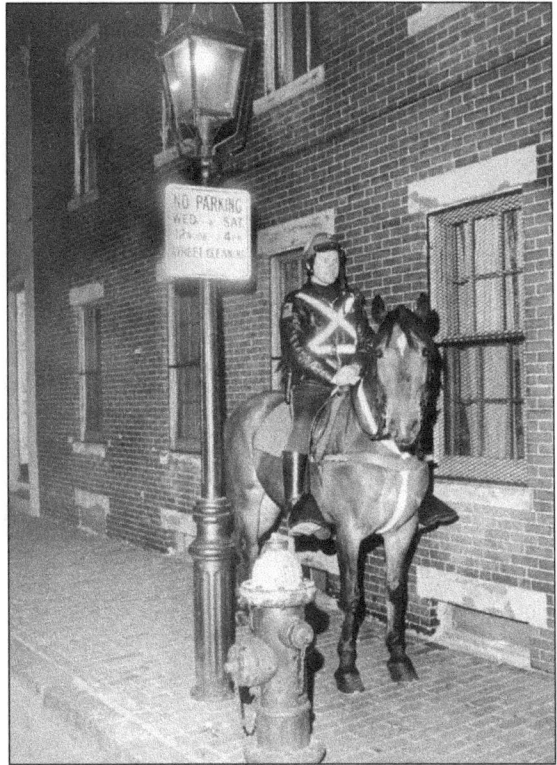

A sergeant assigned to the mounted unit introduces a young boy to his horse before he takes the boy for a ride around the housing development. This was during a community event in November 1975.

Patrolman Robert Howard is shown astride the new steed Orion; this horse is a 10-year-old blue ribbon–winner and was given to the Boston Police Department by 17-year-old Sandra Torngren, of Highland Avenue, Winchester, on May 18, 1949. Orion would serve the Boston Police Department with honor for 10 years.

In 1943, Boston Police mounted patrolman William "Pete" Dooley poses outside the rear of the Boston Police Department's horse stables at Division No. 16. His horse is also smiling for the camera.

The Boston Police Mounted Unit parades down the streets of New York on November 6, 1937, as a guest of West Point. The mounted unit was one of the finest in the country and was invited to perform at many events. The Boston Police Mounted Unit was the nation's first mounted unit.

On May 6, 1978, Mayor Kevin White conducts an inspection of the Boston Police Mounted Unit. Mayor White loved the mounted unit; White himself was even a horse owner. (Courtesy of Joseph Favale.)

Mayor Kevin White thanks two mounted officers after a demonstration they gave for the community of Dorchester on May 6, 1978. (Courtesy of Joseph Favale.)

In another photograph taken on February 6, 1978, Boston Police Mounted Unit officers take a rest after checking areas for homeless people in the Boston Common. (Courtesy of Joseph Favale.)

On February 6, 1978, Boston Police Mounted Unit officers patrol the Boston Common on the lookout for homeless persons during the blizzard of 1978. (Courtesy of Joseph Favale.)

Two mounted officers are shown on February 6, 1978, patrolling the Boston Common in the snowstorm of the blizzard of 1978. The storm, which started on February 5 and lasted until February 7, 1978, dropped more than 27 inches of snow and shut down Boston. (Courtesy of Joseph Favale.)

A mounted officer is watching out for traffic problems in this July 16, 1978, photograph.

In another photograph taken on May 6, 1978, the Boston Police Mounted Unit lines up for inspection by Commissioner Joseph Jordan and Mayor Kevin White. (Courtesy of Joseph Favale.)

Boston Police Mounted Unit officers, from left to right, Columbus Jeannette, Marie Donahue, Jim Leahy, and Sgt. Al McNeal patrol the Government Center on January 22, 1979. (Courtesy of Joseph Favale.)

Lt. Louis E. Lutz (left) and Sgt. Thomas
S.J. Kavanagh (center) display the
Thompson submachine gun that
patrolman Frank Taya is holding on April
29, 1923. These weapons were at the
ready if the May Day riots occurred.

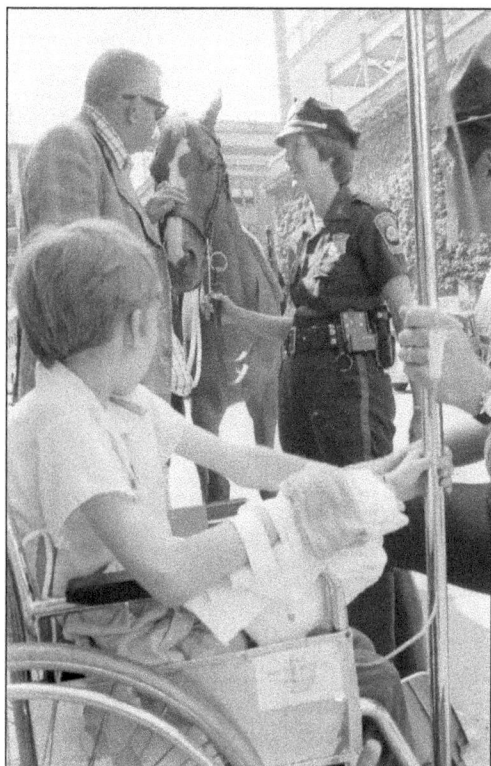

Police officer Marie Donahue was the first
female officer of the Boston Police Mounted
Unit. On April 3, 1979, she is pictured
explaining the upkeep and the work that
the horses do for the city of Boston to a
father as his child looks on. The horses are
one of the biggest community ambassadors
for the Boston Police Department.

On April 3, 1979, police officer Marie Donahue of the Boston Police Mounted Unit is shown pushing a child in his wheelchair. A patient of Boston Children's Hospital, the boy was able to pet the police horse as well as talk to the police officers. (Courtesy of Joseph Favale.)

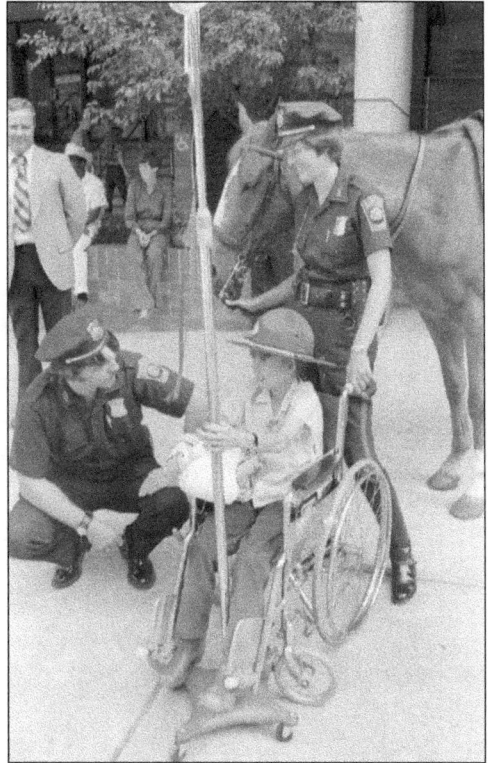

Mayor Kevin White holds the reins of Sgt. Paul Simonetti's horse, as he gets ready to feed him a carrot on November 3, 1980, in Downtown Boston's shopping section. (Courtesy of Joseph Favale.)

Commissioner Joseph Jordan presents a Commissioner's Commendation Plaque to Sgt. Paul Simonetti on November 3, 1980. Sergeant Simonetti is a member of the Boston Police Mounted Unit, and his unit has helped clean up the problems in Downtown Crossing. (Courtesy of Joseph Favale.)

Mounted officer Gene Carroll treats a young girl to a ride on his police horse. This community event was held in Dorchester on August 13, 1980. (Courtesy of Joseph Favale.)

Pictured is Boston Police Mounted Unit officer Gene Carroll; he is taking a small child for a ride on his horse during a neighborhood event in Dorchester on August 13, 1980. (Courtesy of Joseph Favale.)

Four

MOTORCYCLE UNIT

Boston Police motorcycle patrolman Daniel W. Donahue is aboard his Boston Police Indian motorcycle at Braves Field in January 1922. Patrolman Donahue was assigned to District No. 14.

Boston Police Motorcycle Unit members on their Indian motorcycles on the Boston Common are ready to lead the annual parade on October 12, 1923. The annual parade included all command

staff, divisions and commanders, 20 mounted men from Division No. 16, and six patrolmen carrying Thompson submachine guns. Every officer who is not sick partakes in this parade.

Boston Police motorcycle officers are pictured inside the Fens during their shift on January 15, 1921. The patrolman on the right is Daniel W. Donahue; he is standing with an unidentified motorcycle patrolman out of District No. 14.

This photograph, taken November 1921, shows patrolman Daniel W. Donahue aboard his Boston Police Indian motorcycle. He is stopped to talk to a woman while on patrol in the Back Bay.

Motorcycle patrolman Daniel W. Donahue displays his new Indian motorcycle while on patrol in the Back Bay. This photograph was taken on November 21, 1920.

Getting ready for some traffic enforcement on December 15, 1921, patrolman Daniel W. Donahue mounts his motorcycle in Brighton. An unidentified Boston Police patrolman stands in front of Donahue.

Pictured on January 1, 1922, patrolman Daniel W. Donahue stops to take a picture with some civilians before they go about their business. Patrolman Donahue was assigned to Division No. 14, Brighton, and was operating his department-issued motorcycle No. 17.

The Boston Police Motorcycle Unit is shown providing the motorcycle escort and security for Pres. Dwight D. Eisenhower on his visit to Boston on November 11, 1954. This photograph shows the president's motorcade proceeding down Tremont Street.

Boston Police motorcycle patrolman Stockman, patrolman Blood, and motorcycle patrolman Patterson stand in front of the entrance to the Commonwealth Pier on the waterfront in August 1928. This photograph was taken during the unrest of the longshoremen for a possible strike.

Patrolman Kersey Worst models a new motorcycle uniform; officers started to wear the new uniforms in January 1922.

On April 9, 1937, a Boston Police patrolman escorts Helen F. Lothrop and Walter Clark into Boston Police Headquarters where they are being held on an abortion case.

Boston Police detectives clown around with an unidentified Boston Police motorcycle officer on February 14, 1935, as they are escorting him. Looking on are another Boston Police motorcycle officer as well as a detective.

Boston Police TPF motorcycle patrolmen are set up on Brooks Street in East Boston on the afternoon of October 17, 1979. Patrolmen, from left to right, Anthony Cendulo, unidentified, BoBo Olsen, William Crowder, and Edward Eager are ready to escort the school buses back from East Boston High School.

Two Boston Police TPF members on motorcycles are lined up in front of a Boston public school bus on November 12, 1975, ready to escort it from South Boston High School.

On March 10, 1978, a Boston Police officer from the emergency services unit is ready to check on a possible explosive device. The officer is outfitted with equipment to keep him safe from an explosion. Sergeant Rigolio walks with the officer.

The Boston Police Emergency Services Unit, now known as the bomb squad, responds for a call of a possible explosive device. Sergeant Rigolio is helping the officer with his equipment to handle the investigation. This photograph was taken on March 10, 1978.

A Boston Police patrolman assigned to mobile operations patrol (MOP) shows off the Harley sidecar. This photograph was taken on November 10, 1975.

Motorcycle patrolman Lawrence Sullivan, assigned to the tactical patrol force, looks over his burned motorcycle on September 16, 1975. The motorcycle caught fire while he was escorting a school bus during the Boston busing crisis; the Boston Fire Department extinguished it.

A mobile operations patrol officer gets ready to escort a foreign diplomat. As the officer passes on the information to the lead motorcycle on December 13, 1979, he is also making sure the route is covered on Cambridge Street in Downtown Boston.

Members of the Boston Police Tactical Patrol Force are, from left to right, patrolmen Robert O'Toole, Thomas Gleason, and Harold Prefontaine. They are pictured talking about their capture of a Charles Street Jail escapee. The officers returned him to jail on the morning of January 17, 1970. The patrolmen were able to track down the escaped prisoner after a short chase. Later in his Boston Police career, patrolman Prefontaine achieved the highest civil service rank of captain detective. He was also one of the most exceptional instructors at the Boston Police Academy; his knowledge of criminal law was incomparable. Patrolman O'Toole later achieved the rank of deputy superintendent and took command of mobile operations patrol.

Five

K-9 Unit

This photograph, taken on May 7, 1967, is of Boston Police Tactical Force K-9 Gitta biting a young man's raincoat outside the Savoy Theater at a 4:00 a.m. showing of *Casino Royale*. Patrolman Richard Armstead and his dog, Gitta, were able to break up the crowds on Washington Street.

On the morning of January 19, 1963, a German police dog arrives in Boston from West Berlin. An airlines stewardess pets Harro. On the left is the inspector and trainer Hans Repenning of the West Berlin Police Department. Six K-9s were donated to the Boston Police Department by a West Germany magazine to help in its investigation of the Boston Strangler case. This donation established the Boston Police K-9 Unit.

Pictured out of her kennel is Anka, one of six German shepherds being shipped from Germany to Boston to join in the police hunt for the Boston Strangler, who was wanted for attacking and killing women in the city. Helga Scaratti-Girolla of Frankfurt holds tightly to Anka's chain leash. The K-9s were shipped over on February 1, 1963, and were assigned to tactical squads; their ages ranged from nine months to three years. The first handlers were patrolmen William J. Keasley, Robert Armstead, Edward Gaughan, Herbert Craigwell, Albert Kniupis, and Robert Wagner. The Boston handlers had to learn German in order to give the dogs commands. German police inspector and criminal supervisor of the Berlin Detective Bureau Hans Repenning was also sent to train the new handlers. At the time, the commissioner was Edmund L McNamara and the deputy was John T. Howland. Also, police officer Joseph Benson was the Boston Police K-9 trainer for years. This photograph was taken on February 1, 1963.

This photograph was taken on January 23, 1963. The Boston Police Department was plagued by a crime wave, and so it followed the Chicago Police Department's example and acquired police dogs to tackle its problems. Harro von Ustamm, a West Berlin police dog, displays his prowess at fighting criminals during a press demonstration at the Boston Police Department's range. Louis Vuozzo of the Animal Rescue League of Boston wears a padded suit to protect himself against attack by the K-9, who is under the control of his handler, Hans Repenning, of the West Berlin Police Department.

Here, Col. Raymond T. Aguilina, commanding officer of the US Army 3rd Missile Battalion, "Nike Hercules" 5th Artillery, has donated a sentry suit to the Boston Police Department on February 15, 1963. In the suit is Sgt. Charles L. Gagne of the US Army. Pictured at far right is Det. Fred Gaffney of the Boston Police Department. Kneeling is Hans Repenning, the criminal supervisor of the Berlin Detective Bureau, and the dog is Harro von Ustamm. Training was conducted at the US Army headquarters for Nike, located at Merry Mount Park in Quincy.

This photograph, taken on March 29, 1963, shows Hans Repenning walking his dog Harro von Ustamm at Logan Airport for the trip back to Germany. They had completed the training of the new Boston Police K-9s and handlers.

On the morning of January 9, 1963, Hans Repenning leaves Boston Police Headquarters with Mark I, one of six new Boston Police K-9s donated to the Boston Police Department by a West German magazine company. Hans was turning over all the paperwork to the commissioner.

Anka, one of the new Boston Police German shepherds, leads patrolman William Keasley during a search of a building in Charlestown. They were searching for a possible suspect hiding in the warehouse on April 2, 1963.

Patrolmen Herbert Craigwell (left) and William Keasley lead their K-9s, Connie and Anka, at a public demonstration on August 15, 1963. (Courtesy of the *Boston Evening Traveller.*)

Patrolman Gerard O'Rourke, assigned to Division No. 10, watches as K-9 patrolman Joseph Benson gives his dog, Donner, a helping hand into a broken window on a door. The K-9 and patrolmen were able to make an arrest of a suspect who was hiding inside the store on September 19, 1964.

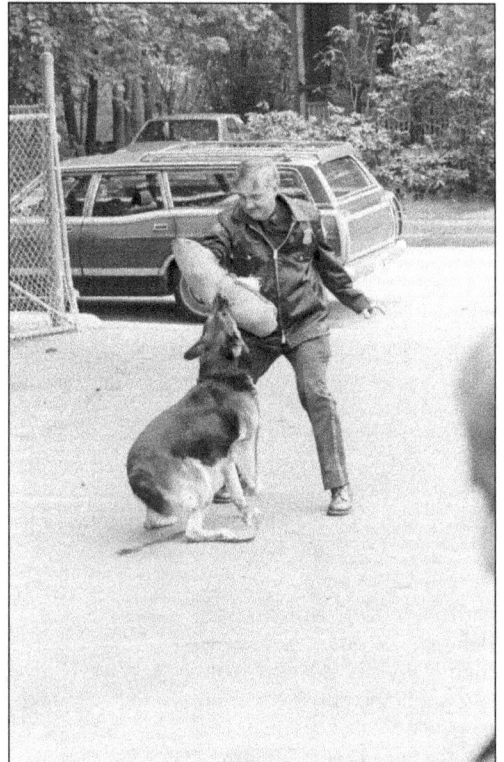

This photograph, taken October 15, 1977, shows a Boston Police K-9 taking a bite out of crime. A K-9 handler is acting as the aggressor during this public demonstration in Dorchester. (Courtesy of Joseph Favale.)

During a community event on October 15, 1977, a Boston Police K-9 handler demonstrates how this K-9 reacts to the sound of a weapon being fired. The K-9 takes a bite out of the arm of the "suspect," who is wearing an arm protector. (Courtesy of Joseph Favale.)

This dog is shown taking down a "suspect" (a police officer) during a demonstration of the Boston Police K-9 Unit on October 15, 1977. (Courtesy of Joseph Favale.)

Here, members of the Boston Police Patrolmen's Association get together with kids from both Roxbury and Dorchester to play games on July 4, 1977.

Here is another photograph taken on July 4, 1977, depicting children of the Roxbury and Dorchester with members of the Boston Police Patrolmen's Association. They are trying to keep their balance in a game during a unity event between the Boston Police and inner-city kids.

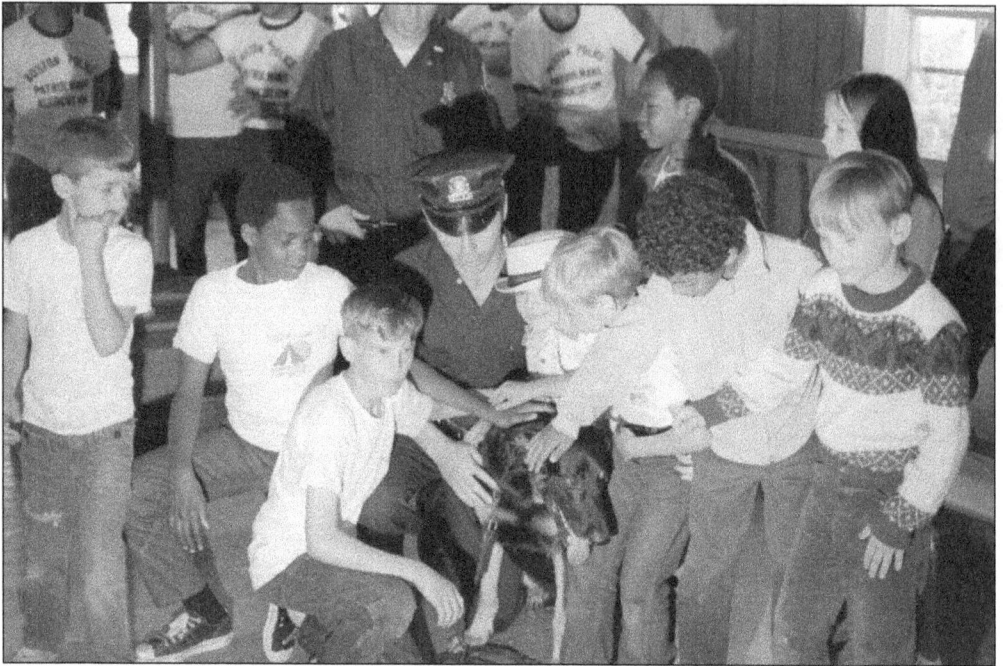

Children of South Boston gather around to pet handler Joseph Benson's dog. Patrolman Benson explains what his K-9 can do for the police department. This photograph was taken at Camp Horizons for Youth on June 12, 1977. (Courtesy of Joseph Favale.)

As the mounted unit officers watch from the sidelines, handler William J. Keasley tells his dog "Down!" during a community event. (Courtesy of Joseph Favale.)

In another photograph, taken on June 5, 1977, patrolman William J. Keasley shows how his K-9 responds to his hands commands during a Boston Police K-9 and Mounted Units demonstration. (Courtesy of Joseph Favale.)

Shown in this photograph, taken June 5, 1977, patrolman William J. Keasley explains how the bond between a dog and its handler helps them do their jobs on the streets of Boston. (Courtesy of Joseph Favale.)

With their K-9s, two of Boston's finest K-9 handlers, patrolmen Arthur Morgan (left) and Robert Armstead, stand ready for action on February 4, 1977.

Six

DEMONSTRATIONS AND TPF

Massachusetts State Guardsmen stand in formation for their assignments in Downtown Boston during the Boston Police strike, which took place in September 1919.

A civilian volunteer wearing a Boston Police badge is shown directing traffic on September 15, 1919, on Summer and Washington Streets in Downtown Boston during the Boston Police strike of 1919.

Boston Police officers check their weapons in with the Boston Police Department's weapons truck before they enter into the Deer Island Prison on March 24, 1972. The officers were called in to patrol the jail when the guards went on strike.

Photographed during a prison guard strike on March 23,1972, Boston Police armor patrolman Krasinski is checking in officers' weapons before they enter into the Deer Island Prison.

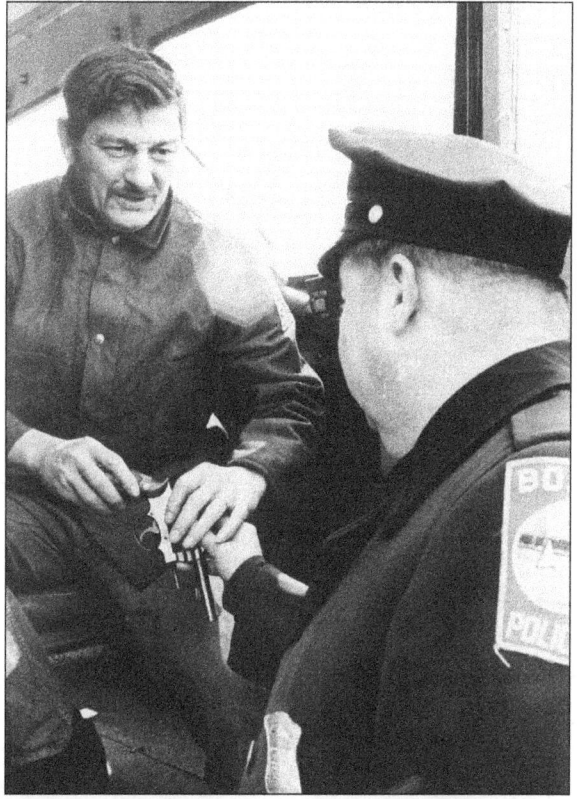

On March 26, 1966, Capt. Daniel Moynihan is wiping his face after being hit by an egg during the antiwar demonstration outside the Arlington Street Church, Boston. This demonstration took place on March 26, 1966. Police officers were called to disperse a crowd of over 1,000; the protestors then started to throw eggs at the officers. Boston Police commissioner Edmund L. McNamara is helping the captain.

Two members of the Boston Police Tactical Patrol Force (TPF) apply a little bit of pressure as they remove an antiwar demonstrator from in front of the John F. Kennedy Federal Building in Government Center on May 8, 1972. More than 1,000 protesters were present at the rally, and more than 100 of them were arrested or removed by members of the TPF.

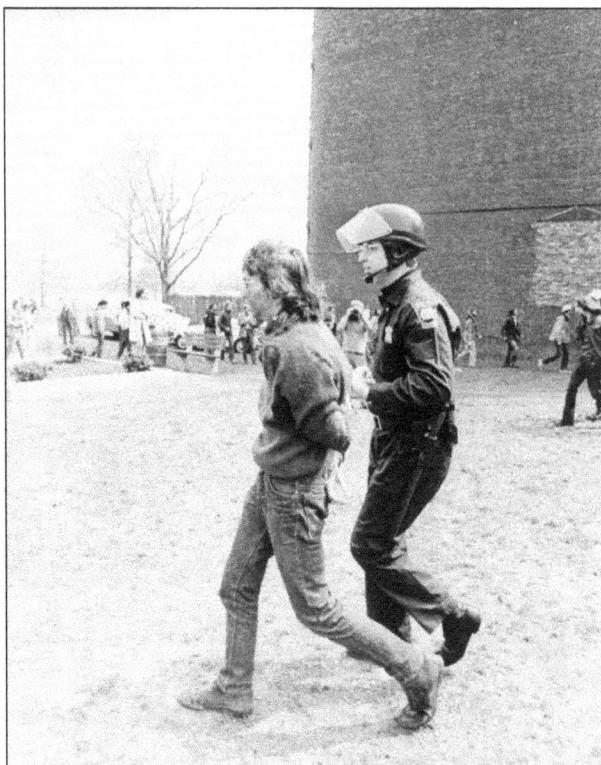

A member of the Boston Police Tactical Patrol Force arrests a demonstrator during the antiwar demonstration on the Boston University campus on May 2, 1973.

Seven

PRESIDENTS AND CELEBRITIES

Members of the Boston Police Traffic Unit (White Hats) provide security for Democratic presidential candidate Sen. John F. Kennedy. Senator Kennedy was in town November 7, 1960.

On August 6, 1963, Pres. John F. Kennedy leaves Boston Children's Hospital after his son Patrick Bouvier Kennedy was born; sadly, Patrick passed away on August 9, 1963. The president (at front of car) is shown with his aide David Powers as they get ready to enter the presidential motorcar. Boston Police provided security for the president.

Pres. John F. Kennedy (right) takes a stroll in Boston's Copley Square and stops to shake the hand of a Boston Police sergeant as he makes his way to the Copley Hotel for a $100-a-plate Democratic fundraising dinner held October 18, 1963. Presidential aide David Powers from Charlestown, Massachusetts, is next to the president. A month later, President Kennedy was assassinated in Dallas, Texas.

Members of the Boston Police Traffic Unit provide security at the Holy Cross Church in the South End of Boston. Jacqueline Kennedy (near center of image), the widow of Pres. John F. Kennedy, is attending a memorial Mass given by Cardinal Richard Cushing of Boston on the morning of January 20, 1964.

On April 23, 1965, Dr. Martin Luther King Jr. is completely surrounded as he leads a civil rights march to historic Boston Common, where he will address a crowd. Dr. King came to Boston to lead the demonstration to protest segregation in schools, jobs, and housing. To his right is his aide Rev. Ralph Abernathy. Boston Police patrolmen were assigned to protect Dr. King. Patrolman Vincent Hayes is assigned to protect Dr. King.

Boston Police commissioner Leo Sullivan (left) shakes hands with bandleader and radio-television performer Lawrence Welk as he arrives in Boston on August 1, 1958. Welk was the producer of *The Lawrence Welk Show,* and his instrumental hits continued to chart through 1973. Welk and his orchestra were in town to perform at the Boston Arena. Commissioner Sullivan was a big fan of Welk and came to the airport to welcome him to Boston.

America's top physical fitness leader, Jack LaLanne, works out Boston's finest tactical patrol force at the YMCA on January 18, 1963. Commissioner Edmund L. McNamara requested that LaLanne come to Boston to train his officers. The men of the TPF took up the commissioner's offer.

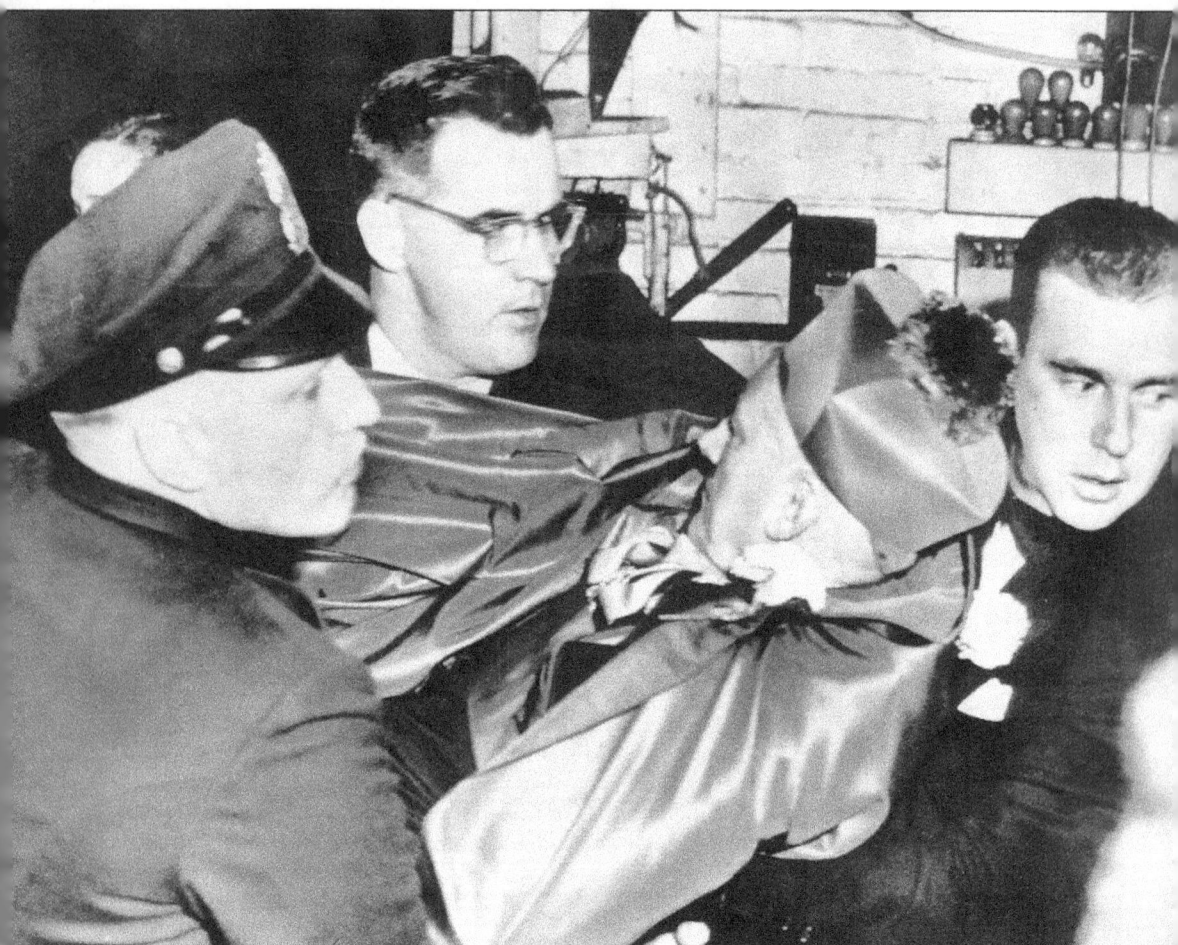

Archbishop Richard J. Cushing of Boston is rushed to the hospital after he fell giving a speech on March 15, 1954. He was carried by police officers. It was discovered that Archbishop Cushing had a kidney ailment, and after a checkup at the hospital, he was taken to his residence in Brighton. Boston Police officers were then assigned to the archbishop full-time.

Eight

LINE OF DUTY

Patrolmen George Hoey (left) and Remi Kennedy of District No. 14 display the weapon they recovered from a suspect they arrested after a shooting in Brighton on December 7, 1956.

Here, Det. Earl Laird (left) and Sgt. John M. White recover a .22-caliber pistol that was used in a shooting on Bromfield Street in Downtown Boston on July 23, 1959.

From left to right, Capt. John F. Petiti, patrolman Edward Silver, patrolman James Welch, and Sgt. Det. Mark Madden of Station No. 11, Dorchester, look over the recovered loot taken from three homes early in the morning on January 27, 1959. The stolen property was valued at $2,500, and it was later learned that the stolen property was actually from a total of 45 different homes. Boston Police arrested a juvenile and were looking for two of his accomplices.

This photograph was taken on October 10, 1957, as Lt. Robert E. Bowes (left) checks a list of patrolmen of the Fields Corner Division No. 11 station with new commanding officer Capt. John F. Petitti. As part of a new patrolman shake-up, they are reviewing a list of transfers.

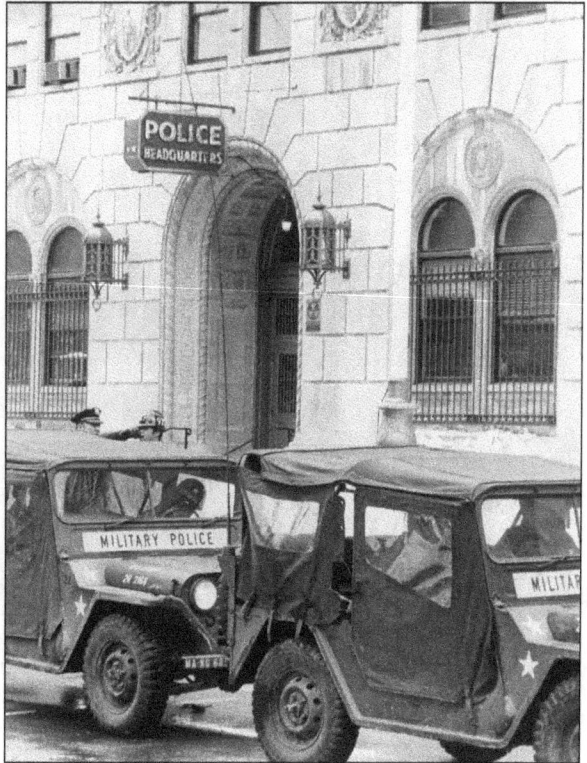

Here, Massachusetts Army National Guard military police Jeeps line up outside Boston Police Headquarters during the blizzard of 1978.

Boston Police stand near the scene where two rookie policemen were shot and wounded as they tried to arrest a man who had double-parked a tractor-trailer truck outside Mr. Kelly's bar on the night of March 2, 1971. Patrolmen Peter Muise and Dennis Ross were both shot after the driver pulled a weapon. Both officers survived their wounds.

The "Pugsley Police Patrol" included seven Pugsley brothers and their father—all on the Boston Police force. They are all pictured after two sons were sworn in on October 21, 1963. Police detective sergeant Arthur Pugsley Sr. congratulates his two recruit sons while their brothers look on. From left to right are Arthur Jr., Stanley G., Ernest A., Sgt. Arthur Sr., Charles H, Robert F., John R., and Richard W. Grandson Jack Pugsley would enter the Boston Police force in 1997.

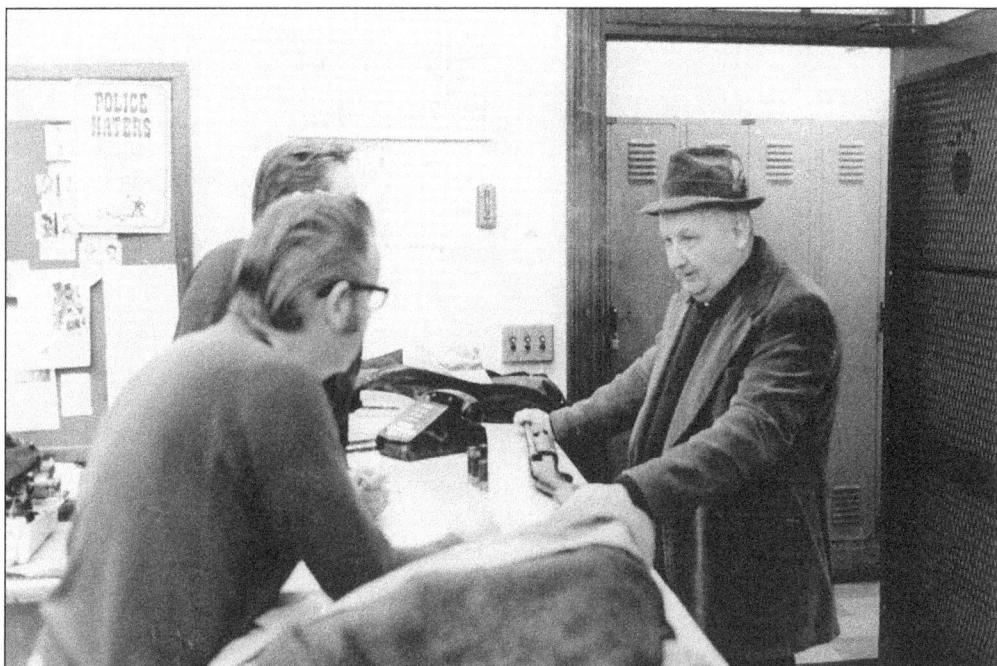

Lt. Edward Connolly signs out a shotgun for his tour of duty on November 9, 1972. Lt. Edward Connolly would rise to the rank of superintendent of the Boston Police Department.

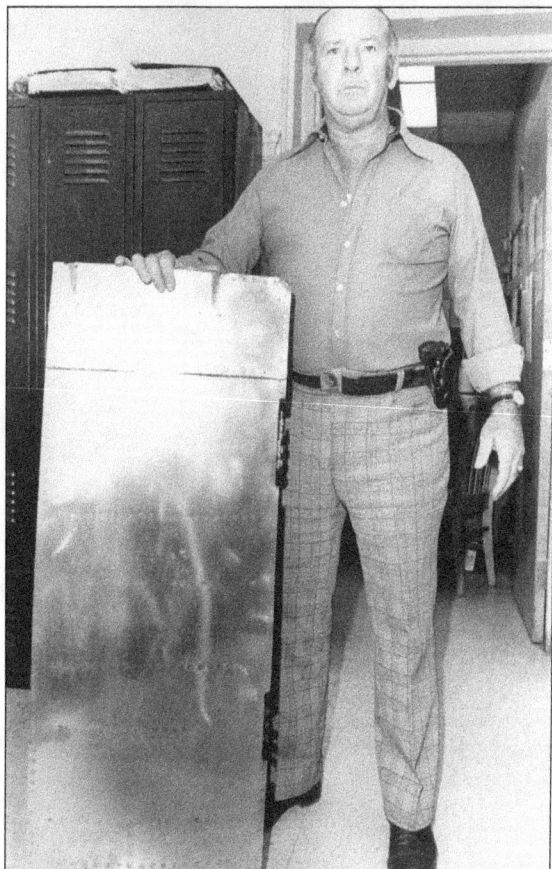

A Boston Police detective displays a shield that was used during a raid on March 10, 1979.

This photograph, taken on December 17, 1976, shows police officer Patricia Reem, the first female motorcycle officer; she was first assigned a scooter and then later a motorcycle. Here, she is writing parking tickets in Downtown Boston.

Here, a lieutenant is relaying a report to police officer Shelia Kaplan for her to type into a police journal on February 4, 1975. All police incident reports were logged in this way.

During the blizzard of 1978, National Guard troops assist the Boston Police Department in Upham's Corner section of Dorchester. The city came to a standstill during this monster snowstorm in February that year. Working 24 hours a day, police officers were forced to take their downtime at the stations.

Superintendent-in-chief Joseph Jordan speaks to members of the command staff at a meeting held on June 6, 1975. To the right of the chief are deputy superintendent Anthony Dinatale, deputy superintendent Peter Donahue, and Lt. Edward Connolly.

Boston Police Department's emergency call center is pictured on September 22, 1973; this is where police officers, cadets, and civilians handle calls and then send them to the dispatcher.

Here, Mayor Kevin White (center) speaks to patrolman Charles Hardy (right), a senior dispatcher for the Boston Police Department. Mayor White came by "the turret," the police communications center, on March 15, 1979, and wanted to see how it functioned.

On January 4, 1976, Lt. Louis Scapicchio (second from left), commander of Boston Police District No. 7, East Boston; Francesca Halloran, the widow of Sgt. Richard F. Halloran; deputy Peter Donahue (second from right), and Ada Mundy (right) unveil a memorial plaque in memory of Sergeant Halloran, who was killed in the line of duty on November 6, 1975, in East Boston. This plaque was placed inside District No. 7. Later, Mayor Thomas Menino, Commissioner Edward Davis, Capt. Robert Cunningham, police officer Robert Anthony, and family members of the Halloran family and members of the Boston Police Department unveiled a granite memorial on November 6, 2007, on Bremen and Bennington Streets where Sergeant Halloran was killed. The man at far left is unidentified.

Boston Police escort the funeral of mounted officer Adelmo Tosi on June 15, 1974, to St. Theresa's Church in the West Roxbury section of Boston. Tosi died while he was an active duty member of the Boston Police Department. Patrolman Tosi's horse, Prescott, with boots placed backwards in the stirrups to honor the fallen rider, walks behind the hearse.

On September 4, 1976, Supt. Joseph Jordan and police chaplain Rev. James H. Lane lead a detachment of Boston Police officers into the Eaton Funeral Home for services for patrolman William R. Beckman. Beckman died in the line of duty after he suffered a severe heart attack while struggling with a prisoner.

Boston Police and police agencies from the state and out of state salute the casket of Det. John James Mulligan on the morning of October 1, 1993, as officers from West Roxbury take it from the hearse. Detective Mulligan was performing a paid detail at a Walgreens drugstore in Roslindale when he was shot in the head four times. At time of the crime, the suspect, who was later arrested, stole Mulligan's gun.

Boston Police officers stand and salute the casket of police officer Charles Israel during his funeral on December 13, 1993. Patrolman Robert Fratalia, the first officer on the left, is shown rendering a hand salute toward the casket. Officer Israel was off duty when he was shot and killed.

Boston Police patrolmen assigned to the traffic division place a wreath at the memorial at Stuart and Tremont Streets dedicated to their fallen brother, patrolman Francis B. "Buck" Johnson. It was near this corner that patrolman Johnson was shot on March 17, 1969, while attempting to apprehend a gunman in a café holdup nearby. The veteran of 23 years of Boston Police service and father of six died of his wounds. The officers proved that, even four years since his passing, he was still not forgotten. Buck's Boston Police badge No. 2794 is attached to the bronze plaque at the corner. The Boston Police Patrolmen's Association dedicated this plaque on March 19, 1973. Shown placing the wreath is patrolman Walter Fahey, a personal friend of patrolman Johnson.

HONOR ROLL

Honoring all members of the Boston Police Department killed in the line of duty

Name	End of Watch	Cause of Death
Watchman Jonathan Houghton	Monday, December 19, 1925	Assault
Watchman David Estes	Thursday, April 27, 1848	Gunfire
Patrolman Ezekiel W. Hodsdon	Sunday, October 18, 1857	Gunfire
Patrolman Cornelius F. Regan	Thursday, January 13, 1898	Duty-related illness
Patrolman Alfred M. Sturdivant	Sunday, September 4, 1904	Gunfire
Patrolman Walter E. Harris	Monday, November 19, 1906	Fall
Patrolman John T. Lynch	Thursday, January 16, 1908	Gunfire
Sergeant Frederick Schlehuber	Thursday, November 10, 1910	Gunfire
Patrolman Richard J. Gallivan	Wednesday, February 8, 1911	Gunfire
Patrolman Albert R. Peterson	Tuesday, October 29, 1912	Gunfire
Inspector Thomas J. Norton	Friday, June 19, 1914	Gunfire
Patrolman Patrick J. Carr	Tuesday, August 1, 1916	Automobile Accident
Patrolman John J. Earle	Saturday, October 21, 1916	Struck by train
Patrolman Joseph C. Reiser	Sunday, January 20, 1918	Gunfire
Patrolman Michael Brennan	Sunday, July 7, 1918	Fall
Patrolman Charles E. Deininger	Thursday, February 13, 1919	Gunfire
Captain Hugh J. Lee	Friday, May 2, 1919	Heart attack
Patrolman Adolph F. Butterman	Monday, June 16, 1919	Gunfire
Patrolman William G. Clancy	Thursday, January 22, 1920	Gunfire
Patrolman Ward M. Bray	Thursday, April 14, 1921	Motorcycle accident
Patrolman Andrew B. Cuneo	Saturday, August 13, 1921	Gunfire
Patrolman Daniel J. McShane	Tuesday, January 31, 1922	Gunfire
Patrolman Peter P. Oginskis	Saturday, May 5, 1923	Automobile accident
Patrolman Joseph E. Gonya	Sunday, October 21, 1923	Gunfire
Patrolman Albert Motroni	Monday, September 22, 1924	Gunfire
Lt. Inspector Benjamin Alexander	Saturday, July 4, 1925	Structure collapse
Patrolman Frank J. Comeau	Wednesday, March 24, 1926	Gunfire
Patrolman Harris B. McInnes	Sunday, July 3, 1927	Gunfire
Patrolman John F. Condon	Thursday, October 7, 1927	Gunfire
Patrolman Herbert D. Allen	Sunday, September 25, 1927	Motorcycle accident
Sergeant Edward Q. Butters	Wednesday, August 14, 1929	Automobile Accident
Patrolman John I. Jackson	Wednesday September 4, 1929	Struck by vehicle
Detective James J. Troy	Monday, January 13, 1930	Gunfire
Patrolman Franklin B. Dreyer	Thursday, April 24, 1930	Gunfire

Patrolman Frederick W. Bartlett	Wednesday, December 10, 1939	Struck by vehicle
Lieutenant Joseph L.A. Cavagnaro	Tuesday, November 17, 1931	Vehicular assault
Patrolman William L. Abbot	Saturday, November 28, 1931	Vehicle pursuit
Sergeant John P.M. Wolfe	Tuesday, December 1, 1931	Automobile accident
Patrolman George J. Hanley	Tuesday, March 20, 1934	Automobile accident
Patrolman James T. Malloy	Monday, June 4, 1934	Struck by vehicle
Patrolman James Brickley	Sunday, November 25, 1925	Automobile accident
Patrolman Daniel A. McCallum	Sunday, May 12, 1935	Automobile accident
Patrolman James D. Hughes	Tuesday, September 10, 1935	Struck by vehicle
Patrolman James B. Roche	Saturday, March 21, 1936	Heart attack
Patrolman James G. McCann Jr.	Tuesday, June 16, 1937	Heart attack
Patrolman Laurence V. Sheridan	Wednesday, July 28, 1937	Assault
Patrolman Walter Baxter	Wednesday, August 4, 1937	Struck by vehicle
Lieutenant Edward Kelly	Thursday, January 14, 1938	Heart attack
Patrolman John H. Manning	Sunday, February 6, 1938	Assault
Patrolman Paul J. Murnane	Friday, September 23, 1938	Heart attack
Patrolman Thomas A. Davis	Thursday, April 13, 1939	Assault
Patrolman Patrick C. Gannon	Tuesday, April 2, 1940	Exposure to toxins
Patrolman Stephen Harrigan	Sunday, January 7, 1941	Heart attack
Patrolman John Lynch	Tuesday, September 19, 1944	Assault
Patrolman Frank B. Callahan	Tuesday, February 20, 1945	Gunfire
Sergeant William F. Healey	Wednesday, October 2, 1946	Gunfire
Patrolman Michael J. Crowley	Friday, May 12, 1961	Motorcycle accident
Patrolman John J. Gallagher	Friday, May 25, 1962	Gunfire
Patrolman James B. O'Leary	Friday, August 2, 1963	Gunfire
Detective George J. Holmes	Wednesday, November 6, 1963	Gunfire
Patrolman Charles A. McNabb	Saturday, November 23, 1968	Gunfire
Patrolman Francis B. Johnson	Monday, March 17, 1969	Gunfire
Patrolman Walter A. Schroeder	Thursday, September 26, 1970	Gunfire
Patrolman Joseph M. Mullen	Monday, December 18, 1972	Automobile accident
Detective John D. Schroeder	Friday, November 30, 1973	Gunfire
Patrolman Donald A. Brown	Friday, May 24, 1974	Gunfire
Detective Francis E. Creamer	Monday, October 7, 1974	Heart attack
Sergeant Richard F. Halloran	Thursday, November 6, 1975	Gunfire
Patrolman William R. Beckman	Wednesday, September 1, 1976	Heart attack
Sergeant Roy Joseph Sergei	Monday, October 26, 1987	Gunfire
Detective Thomas J. Gill	Wednesday, February 10, 1988	Struck by train
Detective Sherman C. Griffiths	Thursday, February 18, 1988	Gunfire
Patrolman Louis H. Metaxas	Sunday, August 27 1989	Fall
Patrolman Jeremiah Hurley Jr.	Monday, October 28, 1991	Bomb
Patrolman Thomas F. Rose	Friday, February, 19, 1993	Gunfire
Detective John James Mulligan	Sunday, September 26, 1993	Gunfire
Patrolman Berisford W. Anderson	Saturday, February 5, 1994	Gunfire

Visit us at
arcadiapublishing.com

www.ingramcontent.com/pod-product-compliance
Lightning Source LLC
Chambersburg PA
CBHW080601110426
42813CB00006B/1368